First American COLONIES

By Yannick Oney

World Discovery History Readers™

SCHOLASTIC INC.

New York • Toronto • London • Auckland • Sydney
Mexico City • New Delhi • Hong Kong • Buenos Aires

First American Colonies

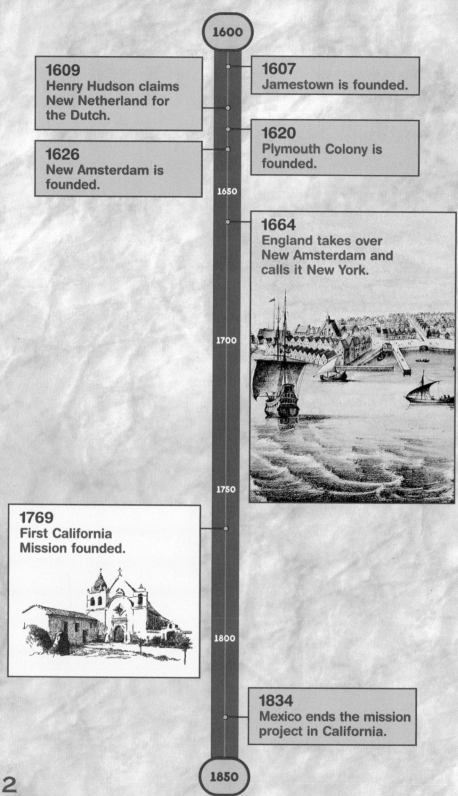

1600

1609
Henry Hudson claims New Netherland for the Dutch.

1607
Jamestown is founded.

1620
Plymouth Colony is founded.

1626
New Amsterdam is founded.

1650

1664
England takes over New Amsterdam and calls it New York.

1700

1750

1769
First California Mission founded.

1800

1834
Mexico ends the mission project in California.

1850

The First Colonies

A long time ago there were no towns or cities in America. America did not have roads, or buildings, or stores as we know them today. The land was rich with trees and wildlife. The only people who lived here were the Native Americans. Then, people from faraway lands came to start towns. These first towns were called **colonies**.

Some of the people who came were businessmen. Others came to practice their religions freely. Some came simply for adventure. Whatever their reasons for coming, they all learned that living in a new land could be harsh. Not only were native people sometimes their enemy, but extreme cold, starvation, and disease were fearful enemies, too.

The stories here are about some of the earliest American colonies and how they survived.

1600

1602

April 1607
104 Englishmen arrive in what is today Chesapeake Bay, Virginia.

May 1607
They begin to build James Fort along the James River.

1604

December 1607
John Smith is captured by the Powhatan tribe and meets Chief Powhatan and Pocahontas.

1606

1608
A fire destroys food at James Fort.

Winter 1609–1610
"Starving Time"
Many settlers die.

Spring 1613
Pocahontas is kidnapped by the settlers.

1612

April 1614
Pocahontas marries settler John Rolfe.

1616

1618

1620

CHAPTER 1

A Rough Beginning for the English
Jamestown, Founded 1607

In 1607, the **Powhatans** lived in a village in present-day Virginia. This Native American Indian tribe was named after their leader, Chief Powhatan. The Powhatans' houses were made of bark and wood. The Indians hunted for their food. They also grew corn.

One day, three English ships with about one hundred men aboard landed near the village. They were businessmen. They came to America to find riches such as furs and gold. After they arrived, a man named John Smith became their leader.

The Jamestown settlers begin building, while the three ships they sailed in—the *Godspeed*, the *Discovery*, and the *Susan Constant*—anchor in the harbor.

"Get ready for winter," John Smith told the men. "Grow crops and hunt for food." But these men wanted to look for gold. They were not interested in starting a colony. John Smith was afraid they would not survive. Some of the men became sick and died. But soon, the survivors began building a fort beside a nearby river. They called it **James Fort**.

John Smith

Chief Powhatan feared that the English would take his tribe's land. He sent his men to get John Smith and bring him to their village. It is believed that the Powhatans held a great feast and a ceremony to welcome John Smith. In the ceremony, the men pretended to capture John Smith, and the chief's eleven-year old daughter, **Pocahontas**, pretended to save him.

Afterward, Pocahontas and John Smith became friends. Pocahontas often visited James Fort. She liked to play there. She taught the settlers native games. She taught them her language, and they taught her English.

The settlers traded with Native Americans for furs such as these to sell to England.

Religious services at Jamestown, 1607

Then a terrible fire destroyed the settlers' food. Pocahontas brought the settlers corn, fish, and fur to help them through their first long winter in Virginia.

A whole year passed. John Smith returned to England. With him away, the Powhatans and the settlers began to fight over the land. It was winter, and the settlers had no food. Many of them died. They called this the **Starving Time**.

This drawing of a Native American village shows crops growing nearby.

Virginia colonists fighting with Native Americans

When the warm weather returned, life got better for the settlers. Families grew, and the settlement grew, too. A town was started outside of James Fort. It was called **Jamestown**. But the Powhatans and the settlers were still enemies. Then the settlers came up with a plan. They decided to capture Pocahontas! They thought if they captured Chief Powhatan's daughter, the Chief would be forced to make peace with them.

Pocahontas captured by the English

Pocahontas,
wife of
John Rolfe,
with their son

Pocahontas stayed in James Fort after she was captured. She wore the same kind of clothes as the other women in the colony. She was given a new name—Rebecca. She married a settler named John Rolfe and had a son. Chief Powhatan would not allow his daughter and her new family to be harmed. At last, Powhatan's men would not attack the settlers.

More families settled in Jamestown and began to farm the rich soil. John Rolfe planted tobacco. The tobacco was sold in England for a lot of money. Tobacco became the "gold" the settlers were looking for. Jamestown had a rough beginning, but in the end, it survived. It became the first permanent English colony in America.

Tobacco plant

The English had tried to settle in America before 1607. In 1586, a group of 120 men, women, and children sailed to Roanoke Island near present-day Virginia. A settler named John White sailed back to England to tell the queen that the colony was doing well. When he returned to the settlement, everyone was gone! Some people think they were killed by Native Americans or simply died from hunger and disease. No one knows for sure. This missing colony is known as the Lost Colony.

Colonists landing on Roanoke Island, 1586

The Mayflower

(A) Roundhouse
The area of the ship where the officers met and ate

(B) Great Cabin
The commander's quarters

(C) Forecastle or fo'c's'l
The cooking area

(D) Lower Deck
The passengers' quarters

(E) Gunroom
Housing for the "stern chasers," cannons used to repel attack

(F) Hold
Main cargo space

CHAPTER 2

The Thankful Settlers
Plymouth Colony, Founded 1620

Unlike Jamestown, Plymouth was not started by businessmen alone. Half of the people who settled Plymouth were **Pilgrims**. These Pilgrims wanted to live in America because they were not allowed to practice their own religion in England. If they did, they were punished, and even sent to jail. Other people came because they could not find jobs or buy land in England. They wanted a better life.

In 1620, about one hundred Pilgrims left England on a ship called the ***Mayflower***. Their trip was terrible. The *Mayflower* got caught in powerful storms, and the passengers were sick and scared. Would they ever see the New World?

Pilgrims coming ashore at Plymouth, Massachusetts

Pilgrims signing the Mayflower Compact, 1620

Then, finally, on November 19, 1620, land was sighted off what is today known as Cape Cod, Massachusetts. On November 21, the Pilgrims signed a paper before they came ashore. The paper was called the **Mayflower Compact**. The Pilgrims agreed to obey their own laws, and not the laws of England.

The Pilgrims explored their new homeland. They decided to start a **colony** in present-day Plymouth. They called it Plymouth **Plantation**. But they had bad luck their very first year.

It was a long, hard winter. The cold weather was very harsh and the Pilgrims did not have enough food. Many people became sick. More than half of the **colonists** died that first winter. Many of the survivors were children younger than sixteen years old.

Finally, the ice melted and spring came. One day, a native named **Samoset** who lived with the **Wampanoag** came to visit the colonists. He spoke English! Then Samoset brought another Native American to the colonists. His name was Tisquantum, and he spoke English, too. His nickname was **Squanto**.

"Welcome, Englishmen," Squanto says as he greets the Pilgrims.

Squanto showed the colonists how to hunt, fish, and grow corn. He was a good teacher. Autumn came and the corn was harvested. Fish was salted and meat was cured for the coming winter. With Squanto's help, the colonists would now have enough food for the winter.

Native Americans taught the settlers about corn. They had white, blue, yellow and red corn.

This photo shows how the colonists cooked. They hung big metal pots over open fires.

"The First Thanksgiving" by Jennie Augusta Brownscombe

The colonists and the Wampanoag gathered for a three-day feast in the fall of 1621 to celebrate the good harvest. There was fish, turkey, and deer meat to eat. There was corn bread, pumpkin and peas, beans, and corn. The colonists bowed their heads and gave thanks for the food and for the help from their Wampanoag friends. Today we call this feast the **First Thanksgiving**.

Like the Jamestown settlers, Plymouth Colony had a rough beginning. But with help from the Native Americans the colony was able to survive. The Pilgrims were also able to practice their own religion freely. America turned out to be a good place to settle.

1520

1524
Giovanni de Verrazano sails into New York Harbor.

1590

1609
Henry Hudson sails on the present-day Hudson River aboard the *Half Moon*.

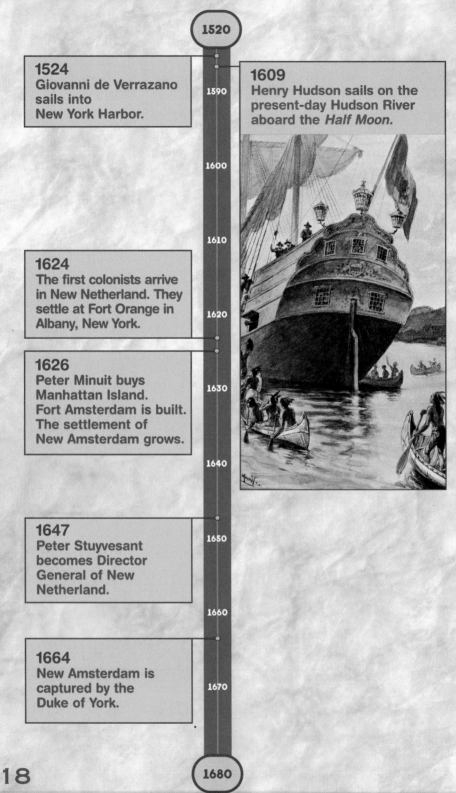

1600

1610

1624
The first colonists arrive in New Netherland. They settle at Fort Orange in Albany, New York.

1620

1626
Peter Minuit buys Manhattan Island. Fort Amsterdam is built. The settlement of New Amsterdam grows.

1630

1640

1647
Peter Stuyvesant becomes Director General of New Netherland.

1650

1660

1664
New Amsterdam is captured by the Duke of York.

1670

1680

CHAPTER 3

The Island Everyone Wanted
New Amsterdam, Founded 1626

Like the Jamestown settlers, the Dutch who came to America were businessmen. They came to make money.

In 1609, Henry Hudson, an English seaman hired by the Dutch East India Company, came to America on his ship the *Half Moon*. He claimed land for the Dutch along the present-day Hudson River. They called this land **New Netherland**.

The Dutch came to America so they could trade for beaver furs. At the time, Europeans were crazy for beaver fur. They paid a lot of money for hats and warm clothes made from the furs.

Beavers were found all over North America. Native Americans used them for fur and for food.

In 1626, Peter Minuit was the Dutch director of New Netherland. He knew of a small island that the natives called "Manhattes." The island had forests and rich soil. Plus, it had good harbors. Ships loaded with precious beaver furs and other goods could easily sail to Europe from the harbor. It was the perfect island for a new Dutch colony. Peter Minuit made a deal with the **Lenni Lenape** tribe, who lived on the island, and bought "Manhattes" from them. The Dutch called their new island **New Amsterdam**.

At first the Dutch and the many Native Americans in the area got along. They wanted to trade with one another, so they tried their best not to fight. The native people traded beaver furs for beads, metal goods, pots, guns, and iron tools.

Dutch merchants trading with Native Americans on Manhattan Island

The Dutch did not go hungry like the Jamestown or Plymouth settlers did. They had brought cows, cattle, horses, sheep, and pigs with them. When they arrived in America, they had milk, cheese, butter, and meat from these animals. Ships from Holland sailed to America regularly with plenty of supplies and food.

The Dutch brought doughnuts and waffles to America.

The Dutch built good homes right away—tall narrow houses made of brick and wood. New Amsterdam had a church, a windmill, and a fort. The Dutch grew grains like wheat and oat on their farms. They also grew vegetables and fruit to feed the people in the colony.

Dutch map of New Netherland and New England in 1630

New Amsterdam in 1667, known today as New York

The Dutch settlement grew quickly. But England was jealous of New Amsterdam's success. In 1664, England's King James II sent two thousand English soldiers to take over New Amsterdam. The Dutch did not have enough soldiers to fight. So they had to give New Amsterdam to England. King James gave the island to his brother, the Duke of York, and the English renamed it **New York**. Today the island is known as **Manhattan**.

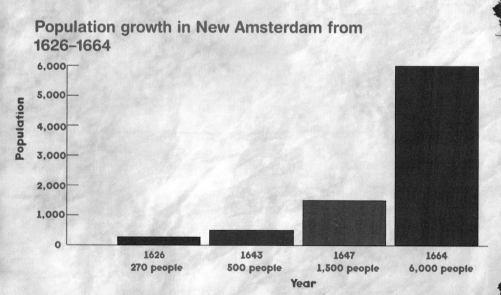

Dutch family having dinner in New Amsterdam

Unlike Jamestown and Plymouth Colony, New Amsterdam did not have a rough beginning. It was not hard for the Dutch to quickly turn New Amsterdam into a lively trading place filled with people who came from many different countries. After the English took over the island, New York grew to be one of England's richest colonies.

Population growth in New Amsterdam from 1626–1664

Year	Population
1626	270 people
1643	500 people
1647	1,500 people
1664	6,000 people

THE CALIFORNIA COAST
UNDER THE MEXICAN RÉGIME.

SCALE OF ENGLISH MILES.

100   200

J. WELLS

Many of the mission sites grew into big cities. San Diego, Los Angeles, San José, and San Francisco all began as Spanish missions. Spain built a chain of twenty-one missions on the coast of California. Each mission was more than a day's journey from the next. The chain of missions was called *El Camino Real*, or the Royal Highway. It was California's first road.

24

CHAPTER 4

The Dream of the Spanish
The California Missions,
First One Founded 1769

The early settlements grew quickly. More and more people came to America. By the middle of the 1700s, there were thirteen colonies in the east, but there was still land in the west that English settlers hadn't ever set foot on. People heard stories that the West was a wild and dangerous place, filled with fierce Native Americans. Who would be the brave ones to settle the West Coast?

Spain decided it would be first. Spain had already settled Mexico, and California is next to Mexico. If Spain settled California, it could easily control **trade routes** along the Pacific coast.

Spain used **missions** to settle the coast of California. Missions were towns run by Spanish priests. In 1769, a priest named Father Junípero Serra was the Mission President. Spain sent Serra and a group of Spanish soldiers on an **expedition** to start the first mission in Southern California.

They left Loreto in Baja, Mexico, for the long ride north. It took them more than three months to reach what is today known as San Diego, California. Father Serra wanted to build a mission right away. But he and his men needed supplies and food first.

Father Junípero Serra

They waited for a ship to come from Mexico. It would bring them what they needed. They waited almost eight months! Where was the ship? They were running out of food.

Like the Jamestown and Plymouth colonists, Serra and his men were in danger of disease and starving to death. Many became sick and died. The men decided they could not wait any longer. They wanted to go back to Mexico. Finally the ship came. Work on the first California mission began.

The work was not easy. The priests, known as **padres**, had the job of making sure the native people would live and work at the missions and pray to a Christian god. Spain believed that if they **converted** the native people to Christianity, they would want to work for the Spanish. The *padres* taught them how to speak, read, and write Spanish. They gave them gifts of beads, clothing, and blankets. Soon the Native Americans did most of the work for the Spaniards.

The mission buildings formed a square. The doors to the buildings all faced the center of the square, where there was a courtyard with a fountain. The church was the largest building. People at the missions farmed and grew their own food and raised their own cattle.

Native American ringing bell for sunrise Mass at Pala Mission

A mission was built around a courtyard with a fountain. The largest building was the church. Other buildings had rooms for cooking, doing office work, making crafts, and storing supplies. The land just outside the mission was used for farming and grazing cattle. Some of the missions had forts called *presidios*. Soldiers protected the missions and the nearby native villages.

Many native people did not like being told how to live and which god to pray to. They did not want to be forced to work at the missions. Many of them rebelled and fought the Spanish. Troubles continued for a long time. The missions lasted almost sixty-five years.

The *padres* showed the natives how to bring water to their fields of crops. This is known as irrigation.

By 1850, Spain no longer ruled Mexico, and California was now part of the United States. The Spanish priests left the missions. People claimed the mission land so they could have their own ranches and farms. The natives were now made to work the land for the new landowners, but they were not paid for the work they did. In 1861, the missions were given to the Catholic Church.

Over time, the empty mission buildings fell apart. But thanks to the success of the missions, Europeans and other people decided to move to California. The missions helped people see that it was possible to farm the dry land and raise cattle. They discovered that California was a place filled with warm sunshine and beautiful mountains. Ships could sail to Asia and all over the world from California's golden coast.

Jamestown, Plymouth, New Amsterdam, and the California missions were all started in different places, at different times, and for different reasons, yet all these settlers had one thing in common. They all helped change America and bring thousands of new people to live and work in the new land. Trees were cleared, crops were planted, buildings were built, businesses were started, and laws were made. The land and its native peoples were changed forever.

The mission at Santa Barbara

Glossary

Colonies: Settlements in distant territories that remain under the rule of the parent country.

Colonists: People who live in a colony.

Converted: Changed from one religion or belief to another.

Expedition: A group of people that makes a journey.

First Thanksgiving: A three-day feast held in the fall of 1621 that celebrated the Plymouth colonists' successful harvest after their first harsh winter in North America.

James Fort: A fort built in 1607 by English settlers on what is now Jamestown Island, Virginia.

Jamestown: The town started outside of James Fort by settlers and their families.

Lenape: Native American nation who inhabited Manhattan during the 16th and 17th centuries.

Manhattan: An island originally known as Manhattes by the Lenni Lenape Native Americans. When the Dutch settled the island, they called it New Amsterdam. It was renamed New York by the English after the city of York in northern England. Today, the island of Manhattan is part of New York City.

Mayflower: The ship that brought more than one hundred Pilgrims to the New World.

Mayflower Compact: A document written and signed by the first group of colonists of Plymouth Colony. Colonists agreed they would obey their own laws, and not the laws of England.

Missions: Places where people who came to spread religion lived and worked.

New Amsterdam: The island purchased by the Dutch from the Lenni Lenape in 1626. Today, this island is called Manhattan.

New Netherland: Territory along the present-day Hudson River that was claimed by the Dutch in the early 17th century.

New York: A common name for New York City, the largest city in New York State, and the United States. New York City is located in southeastern New York at the mouth of the Hudson River.

Padres: Spanish priests.

Pilgrims: Some of the settlers who founded Plymouth Colony. They came to America from England so they could practice their religion freely.

Plantation: A large farm or estate on which crops, especially cotton, are cared for and harvested by workers who often live there.

Pocahontas: The daughter of the chief of the Powhatan tribe. She befriended the English settlers at James Fort and helped to bring peace between the Native Americans and the settlers.

Powhatans: A native tribe in eastern Virginia named for the chief and founder, Powhatan.

Samoset: The first Native American to make contact with the Pilgrims in 1621.

Squanto: One of the first Native Americans who helped the Pilgrims during their first winter.

Starving Time: The period between September 1609 and May 1610 during which approximately five hundred James Fort settlers died from lack of food.

Trade routes: Lanes of travel between two or more places where the exchange of goods takes place.

Wampanoag: Native American people who lived in what is now south-eastern Massachusetts in the early 17th century.